START STRONG

Simple Habits to Thrive in Any Season of Life

Bruce Downes

Start Strong: Simple Habits to Thrive in Any Season of Life
© 2022 by Bruce Downes

ISBN 978-1-7334702-9-2

For more information contact
Bruce Downes Ministries
PO Box 55750
Phoenix, AZ 85078
(602) 612-9705
BruceDownes.org

START STRONG

Simple Habits to Thrive in Any Season of Life

DEDICATION

Thank you to my incredible staff.
So many people have been affected by your
love of God and your resilience and that
when we face the inevitable challenges that come,
you lift to the next level and from there Start Strong.

CONTENTS

INTRODUCTION

COMMITTING YOUR PLANS

This is going to be a magnificent season of your life.

Why do I say that, and how do I know it?

As Christians, our goal is to grow closer to God in our everyday lives. If we can get closer to God, we begin to resemble God more in how we live, think and love. God has created us for that.

Jesus told us that in life, you would have problems. There are no guarantees that problems will go away because you are a committed Christian, but instead, you receive the power to live amid both the joy and the struggles of life.

It is time to receive this power and start living strong in this next season.

I always have big plans, and I have got to admit that I have got many plans for this next season, and the Scriptures give us some indication as to how we are meant to approach our plans.

You and I are uncovering how we can start something brand new this season. The principles of this book about starting strong apply to starting new things at any time in your life. We all want good results in our actions, and none of us ever want to fail, so let us commit to starting strong together.

In Proverbs 16, verse 3, it says,

> *Commit your work to the Lord, and your plans will be established.*

The writer of Proverbs says that as you start today, submit or commit your plans to God. Commit to God what you are doing and how you will go forward. Commit all the details and each of the steps you will take.

What are your plans right now? I have plans and want them to succeed, so I want to commit them to God. I want to say, 'God, these are my plans. I commit them to You so that You would bring Your blessing upon them.'

In Psalm 37, verse 5, it says this:

> *Commit your way to the Lord; trust in him, and he will act.*

If we commit our plans to God, we can trust and be confident that He will act for us.

If it is something new that God wants me to do or establish – in my case, setting up a thousand groups of people around the world who are growing in faith, reaching out and serving other people in their local areas across different countries – if that is to work – God has got to turn up, and God has got to do it.

What do the Scriptures say?

> *Commit your way to the Lord; trust in him, and he will act.*

So, in your business or study, what are your plans? Commit them to God.

In your marriage or family, what are your plans? Commit them to God.

In your health, fitness, and exercise? Commit those plans to God.

When I commit something to God, I hear God saying back to me, "Bruce, that's a good plan, but let Me show you My plan." And then I realize, "Wow that is even better."

God has a way of tweaking the thoughts within us to make them even better.

Sometimes God plants something brand new in us.

When I was younger, I used to think life was about achieving things and, indeed, that is important, but I have also come to see that for me at my age, and where I am at with things, starting strong means I need to learn to be still.

I wish someone had told me this when I was twenty because, to be honest with you, if I had learned to be still during activity, I think I would have been able to do a lot more. I think I wouldn't have made as many mistakes in my life, and I would have been a lot happier at times than I was.

Scripture tells us that by committing your plans, ideas, thoughts, and the direction you will go next to God, you will prosper, and God will bless you throughout the season you are in.

As we begin, let us pray together and commit this next season to God.

Loving Father, You see me as I read or listen right now. Father, in the name of Jesus, through the power of Your Holy Spirit, bless my plans for the next season. Guide me also if I don't have any plans right now. Lord God, allow me and show me how you mean to grow more deeply within me.

I commit these plans to You. Lord, I am open to your comments. I am open to Your guidance. I am open to you telling me to go this way or go that way. I am open to You blessing the plans and establishing them to succeed. If there are things that you have for me that I am not even thinking about, Father, please convict me, show me, guide me, and lead me.

Jesus, be my Savior and Lord. Redeem my life through voice and Your action into my heart. Holy Spirit, be the power of God upon this season or year. Bless this season in our homes, cities, towns, villages, and countries. Wherever I am, I commit this time into Your hands, and I thank You that you're with me. Thank You, and Father, I make this prayer in the name of Jesus, through the power of Your Holy Spirit. Amen.

CHAPTER ONE

THE PERSON GOD WANTS
YOU TO BE

What will this next season or year bring to you? I know I make many decisions to go in a particular direction in my own life at the start of the year. I don't do them as New Year's resolutions because that is too quick after Christmas for me, but I put some time into thinking about where I will be with my staff. I often ask them this question: what do you think we'll be at the end of the year? I've done that for years and it is fascinating what people say.

If I have learned anything in life, it is this. **'You never become whom you hope to become; you only become what you do.'**

I will repeat that. You never become whom you hope to become; you only become what you do. As I have gotten older, I hope to become someone in a deeper relationship with God. I want to be someone God would look at and say, 'I am proud of you.'

I will never become that person unless I do certain things to get me to that point. With my children, who are a lot younger and are setting out in life, the things they do now will dictate the year or season that they will have. And for them, God is asking different sets of questions than of me. He is asking questions of me and He is asking questions of you.

At the beginning of this season or year, we ask, 'Am I the person God wants me to be? And what do I need to do to get there?'

I was raised in a Carmelite parish, and the Carmelites are very much focused on prayer, and that is really where I am trying to lead you in this journey we have started. I talk to myself in this as much as I speak to you. It is about you and me developing a more profound relationship with God in prayer.

If someone said to me, 'What is the purpose of life?' I would say to be happy, but I don't mean happy in a self-centered way, but happy in the sense of content and happy in being what God has called me to be.

We know that God is calling us into a relationship with Him and having an intimate love life with Him. In a sense, that is the essence of prayer. In Psalm 1, verse 2 it says:

> *But their delight is in the law of the Lord, and on his law, they meditate day and night.*

In other words, happy people see what God says to them and has revealed in their hearts, then meditate on what has been revealed.

There are some of you that God is calling to be successful in business.

There are some of you that God is calling to rest in Him as you get older and sit with Him and know Him and be drawn into an ever-deepening relationship with Him.

There are some of you that God is asking to do certain things in your marriage or work or to do certain things in your life.

The following are all very spiritual things:

- How you invest your money.
- How you spend your time.

- How you love your children.
- How you work and work hard at what you do.

These are the things that make us who we are, and we have a relationship with God through them and in them. So, the very ordinary things like how we look after our home and the workplace are very spiritual things that matter to God.

When we listen to God and hear God speak about these areas of our lives, we decide that is what we want to do. In a sense, we delight in it. The Scripture says, *'That is where happiness is.'*

And then it says,

> *They are like trees planted by streams of water, which yield their fruit in its season. And their leaves do not wither. In all they do, they prosper.*

They prosper!

In other words, the Scripture says that if we meditate upon whom God is calling us to be, as we pray for what God is asking of us in our daily lives, we experience happiness.

Even when circumstances occur around us like pandemics, hardship, like the cruelness and meanness of people to us, as we respond to those things, there is more profound happiness or peace that sets upon us.

I am trying to help you to encounter Jesus in your everyday life.

As we start into this new season or year, why don't you think to yourself, how does God want me to live? What would be my ultimate life? Not what things do I want, but what is the ultimate thing? The life that I would stop and say, 'I think that is what God is saying and I am going to delight in that.'

Take that to prayer, talk to God about it, and it will transform the way you think, the way you live, and the way you go about your day. You will encounter the presence of God in a real way.

We all need prompting moments in our lives that help us go back and say from now on...

I want to encourage you in prayer. Keep saying to yourself, 'God, what are you saying to me? How are you speaking to me about the ordinary things of life that are also the most spiritual in my life?'

A final thought we shouldn't go to church on Sunday, and then the rest of our life is different from what our church life is.

Sometimes family life can be challenging, can't it? Sometimes work-life could be tough, can't it? We take that to church. As you sit down at home by yourself, and you can have church at home in a sense where you are, before the presence of God, or wherever you do that, you have to take the honesty of who you are to God every day.

We are not meant to spend 15 minutes of prayer a day when we are doing our 'God stuff,' but for the rest of the day, we are not. God wants to be in our life all the time, and He transforms us and changes us as we concentrate on Him.

So, ask yourself the question, 'Whom does God want me to be, and am I becoming that? I will never become whom I hope to become, I will only become what I do.

What do I need to do and pray about today if I am going to delight in the Lord for me in my life?

CHAPTER TWO

A STRONG START

I remember once deciding for New Year's Eve that I was giving up unhealthy food to lose weight because that is what pretty much all my new year's resolutions are about. I am always trying to lose weight. I was giving up ice cream, and I remember midnight came, so I made sure I ate ice cream at five to twelve before the deadline. Do you know how you indulge just before you give something up? And then, at twelve-fifteen, I remember standing in the kitchen with this bowl of ice cream in my hands, and I was eating it, and Rosemary walked by and said, "I thought you were giving up ice cream." I looked down and said, "How did this get here?" Then Rosemary tells me she saw me walk to the fridge, get the ice cream out, and put it in a bowl.

Have you ever just done something automatically that you weren't aware that you were doing?

I was listening to someone give a talk the other day, and as they were talking, every third or fourth phrase was, 'Um.' I am confident that the speaker was unaware that they were doing it. There are so many things like this that we do on autopilot. So rather than making a resolution that I am not going to keep, I decided that I would come at this differently because so many of us want significant change in our lives.

We don't want change. We want a more profound change or more significant change for the better. So, I wanted to start this book called Start Strong, not Becoming Strong, but start strong right at the line to finish well.

I remember running in the 400 meters race at school and taking off from the start line. Four hundred meters was one entire lap around the oval. I took off, and at the 200-meter mark, I heard the commentator in the background saying my surname, 'Downesy,' which was what they used to call me at school. I hear them say, "Downesy is so far in front; this is going to be a record." I remember getting to the finish line and falling just this side of the line. You see, I didn't finish well because I had not started strong enough. I went too hard, too fast, and ran out of steam before the end.

Now I am not a motivational speaker or writer. I would love to be, but I am just not. I am not a 'think positive,' and in your future, you will be a better kind of speaker or writer. I am certainly not a 'you can do it,' coach-like speaker and writer.

I will take a passage of the Bible, and I will try and bring it to life for you. I will let it speak to you because God speaks to us through the Scriptures, and you will get a lot more out of that than if I say or write something intelligent or inspiring.

We can think the Bible is just one book, but it is a whole series of miniature books contained in one book. The word Bible comes from the original word 'biblios,' meaning text.

I want to look at this whole subject of how you start strong by looking at a person in the Bible that some people argue was the most outstanding leader in all human history. This man's name was Moses. Some of you might ask, wasn't Jesus the best leader ever, but Jesus is in a category all by Himself.

We will start reading in Exodus 1, verse 8, and as we tell this story, we will talk about how we can start strong so that what we decide to do becomes a reality.

> *Now a king arose over Egypt who did not know Joseph.*

Let's just stop there for a second. This is not Joseph, Mary's husband, and Jesus' earthly father. This is Joseph, who lived back in the early times of the Scriptures and was an Israelite or a Hebrew person. Yet, he rose to be the second most powerful man in all of Egypt.

At that time, Egypt was the most powerful nation in the world. Joseph was known by the Pharaoh or King, who was all-powerful. The Pharaoh had the kind of power that he could put a person to death on a whim. It is quite amazing that Joseph rose to be the number two, even though he was not an Egyptian.

We will be reading about a few centuries ago when a new King or Pharaoh arose over Egypt who didn't know Joseph and how popular he was.

In verse 9, the king said to his people,

> *"Look, the Israelite people are more numerous and powerful than we."*

In verse 10, it says,

> *"Come, let us deal shrewdly with them, or they will increase and, in the event of war, join our enemies and fight against us and escape from the*

land." Therefore, they set taskmasters over them to oppress them with forced labor. They built supply cities, Pithom and Rameses, for Pharaoh. But the more they were oppressed, the more they multiplied and spread so that the Egyptians came to dread the Israelites. The Egyptians became ruthless in imposing tasks on the Israelites and made their lives bitter with hard service in mortar and brick and every kind of field labor. They were ruthless in all the tasks that they imposed on them.

So, the Egyptians captured the Hebrews or Israelite people. These people had grown up among them, but the Egyptians were ruthless in imposing tasks on them. Meanwhile, the Israelites became physically stronger because they were doing strenuous work. It got to the point where the Egyptians feared their strength, and the whole economy of Egypt became dependent upon these slaves. The Egyptians became worried that they would get overthrown by the Israelites who were their slaves.

This is a great story. The king directs the midwives, the women who helped give birth to the Israelite boys and girls that if there is a little Israelite boy born, he must be thrown into the Nile River, but the little girls were allowed to live.

This is the directive. However, the midwives didn't do as they were directed. They feared God more than they feared Pharaoh, so they refused to do what was asked of them.

In Exodus, chapter 2, verse 1, it says,

Now a man from the house of Levi went and

married a Levite woman. The woman conceived and bore a son, and when she saw that he was a fine baby, she hid him for three months. When she could hide him no longer, she got a papyrus basket for him and plastered it with bitumen and pitch; she put the child in it and placed it among the reeds on the bank of the river. His sister stood at a distance to see what would happen to him.

This decree came out that all baby boys were to be killed. So, the mother of Moses hid her little boy. She realized that if the babies started making noise, they got noticed, so she decided to put her little boy into a basket and sail him down to where all the princesses of Egypt were. In verse 5, it says:

The daughter of Pharaoh came down to bathe at the river while her attendants walked beside the river. She saw the basket among the reeds and sent her maid to bring it. When she opened it, she saw the child. He was crying, and she took pity on him. "This must be one of the Hebrews' children," she said.

Now, this is interesting. The baby's mother wonders how to keep her little boy alive and what would happen if she could get her little boy to live with the very people trying to kill her people's little boys. So, she came up with a strategy to float him down the river. She put a lid on the basket and hoped they would look after him. The princesses picked up the basket, lifted the lid off, saw this baby, and wanted to protect him even though they knew it was a little Hebrew boy.

The princess took the baby home and sent for someone to feed the baby. His mother is the one who comes and feeds him and raises him, and then when he is at the right age, she presents him to Pharaoh's home. So, it is Pharaoh who raises the boy under his roof. The princess named the boy Moses, which means "drew him out of the water."

The mother of Moses gave him the strongest start she could in floating him down the river towards the Pharoah's palace. How difficult that must have been for her, and yet her plan to save her child meant that Moses ended up in the palace, which led to him becoming a leader who could lead the people of Egypt. Starting next season, are there areas where you need to make a hard decision or sacrifice more for a better outcome? Do you want to lose weight but don't want to eat less or exercise? Do you want a better job but don't want to undergo training or expand your skills? Do you want to be a better mother, parent, or friend, but you don't want to change how you do things?

How can you move into new seasons with strength and confidence?

CHAPTER THREE

TURNING IN THE RIGHT DIRECTION

Because his mother decided to float Moses in a basket towards the palace, he grew up close to the Pharoah and had access to training and leadership and the best of everything.

The story continues, in verse 11, it says:

> *One day, after Moses had grown up, he went out to his people and saw their forced labor. He saw an Egyptian beating a Hebrew, one of his kinsfolk. He looked this way and that, and seeing no one, he killed the Egyptian and hid him in the sand. When he went out the next day, he saw two Hebrews fighting; and he said to the one who was in the wrong, "Why do you strike your fellow Hebrew?" He answered, "Who made you a ruler and judge over us? Do you mean to kill me as you killed the Egyptian?" Then Moses was afraid and thought, "Surely the thing is known." When Pharaoh heard of it, he sought to kill Moses. But Moses fled from Pharaoh. He settled in the land of Midian and sat down by a well.*

Moses murdered an Egyptian and then discovered that Pharaoh was trying to punish him by killing him. So, Moses fled from Pharaoh because he had the authority to take a person's life. Moses then becomes a shepherd, and in verse 23:

> *After a long time, the king of Egypt died. The Israelites*
> *groaned under their slavery and cried out. Out of*
> *slavery, their cry for help rose up to God. God heard*
> *their groaning, and God remembered his covenant*
> *with Abraham, Isaac, and Jacob. God looked upon*
> *the Israelites, and God took notice of them.*

The Pharaoh who had banished and tried to kill Joseph dies, and a new Pharaoh takes over. The people of Israel who were captured and oppressed by the Egyptians begin to cry out to God, 'God, would you save us? God, would you help? Would you be merciful to us?'

Scripture says,

> *God heard their groaning, and God remembered the*
> *covenant he'd made with their ancestors.*

The word 'covenant' means agreement, and it is one of the critical aspects of understanding how God loves us and deals with us. A covenant means an agreement that is binding. It is like the two of you become one. God has made this commitment, and He remembers that He said to them, 'I am going to be your God. You are going to be my people. I am going to look after you.'

One day, Moses is going about his job looking after sheep. In chapter 3 it says,

> *Moses was keeping the flock of his father-in-law*
> *Jethro, the priest of Midian; he led his flock beyond*
> *the wilderness and came to Horeb, the mountain of*

God. There the angel of the Lord appeared to him in a flame of fire out of a bush; he looked, and the bush was blazing, yet it was not consumed. Then Moses said, "I must turn aside and look at this great sight and see why the bush is not burned up."

Moses is doing his job looking after sheep, then suddenly, a bush begins to burn, and he looks straight at it.

When we are looking for a new direction in our life, it is not immediately in front of us, sometimes it is to the side of us, but we must turn toward the voice, the direction, the new thing, that God might be speaking to us.

Sometimes, God speaks in obscure ways. He speaks through people, through circumstances or events. In verse 3, it says:

Then Moses said, "I must turn aside and look at this great sight and see why the bush is not burned up."

How many of you have had things in your lives that you are doing where you look back and say, 'God, I wish I had not missed that opportunity.'

When God saw that Moses 'turned aside' to see the bush, He called to him out of the bush, *"Moses, Moses."* So, God gives him a sign that he must turn and look. Moses must be distracted from the thing he has his mind focused on.

We are so busy raising our children; we forget to hear the voice of God or the opportunities that God gives us. We are so busy with our careers. We are so busy being us that we don't pause to listen.

When the Lord saw that he had turned aside to see, God called to him out of the bush, "Moses, Moses!" And he said, "Here I am." Then he said, "Come no closer! Remove the sandals from your feet, for the place on which you are standing is holy ground."

When we hear something and 'turn aside' towards God, He speaks to us through our circumstances and our lives. God speaks to us through our marriages that end. He speaks to us through a movie that we watch. God speaks to us through a mistake we have made. God speaks to us through the success we have. When God speaks to us, He doesn't talk with audible words. That is a holy, sacred moment when God speaks because it changes everything.

CHAPTER FOUR

YOUR PROMISED LAND

G od said to Moses, "I have seen all of the trouble that they are in. I have seen their groaning. I have seen how they've been treated, and I am going take them to a land flowing with milk and honey." We wouldn't use that phrase now, but it means a very prosperous land. "The land I am going to take them or the 'promised land' is already occupied."

> Then he said, "Come no closer! Remove the sandals from your feet, for the place on which you are standing is holy ground." He said further, "I am the God of your father, the God of Abraham, the God of Isaac, and the God of Jacob." And Moses hid his face, for he was afraid to look at God. Indeed, I know their sufferings, and I have come down to deliver them from the Egyptians and to bring them up out of that land to a good and broad land, a land flowing with milk and honey, to the country of the Canaanites, the Hittites, the Amorites, the Perizzites, the Hivites, and the Jebusites. The cry of the Israelites has now come to me; I have also seen how the Egyptians oppress them.

For most of us, if we want to have a better future, our future is already occupied with other things. Our future is already occupied with busyness, distractions, and things that have already happened with family or our career. Our promised land often is already occupied with other things.

> *The cry of the Israelites has now come to me; I have also seen how the Egyptians oppress them. So come, I will send you to Pharaoh to bring my people, the Israelites, out of Egypt."*

God says, "I am coming down to do it," and then He says, "You Moses will do it." Whenever God wants to do something new, He picks a person.

> *But Moses said to God, "Who am I that I should go to Pharaoh and bring the Israelites out of Egypt?"*

In other words, "No, no, no. How can you pick me? Look at my credentials. Look at who I am."

> *And God said, "I will be with you; and this shall be the sign for you that it is I who sent you: when you have brought the people out of Egypt, you shall worship God on this mountain."*

Let's look at Moses's life. He was born when the Pharaoh has directed midwives to kill all baby boys because of politics and power. His mother gives him up, and she decides to put him in a basket and float him down to where the princesses from the Pharaoh's palace bathe. Moses then lives the rest of his life at the Pharaoh's palace until he murders someone, then he runs away and becomes a fugitive.

Now imagine what it would have been like going from living in the most important palace in the known world to being out in the field looking after sheep.

Imagine that… but I walked down the aisle, and I said to this girl who was dressed in white, "I am going to love you with my whole heart." I started that career, and I was doing well. I was driving down the street, and a mess hit me. I ended up with a boss who had problems, who persecuted me…

Who has been brutal to someone else? Moses gets in a fight, and he kills someone. In a moment, his life changed. He runs from the problem and the pharaoh, and then one day, he has this 'burning bush' experience. That would be weird. Then God says to Moses out of the bush, "I want you to get my people out of Egypt."

Moses stands there at the burning bush and has a long debate with God. In this long debate with God, Moses says, "I can't do it. Who am I? I don't know who you are, God, and besides, I am not a good speaker. Anyway, what authority do I have?"

Moses looks for excuses not to do what God is putting in front of him. He is living a life that he has now become accustomed to where he looks after sheep that just stand around on the hill. He takes them out in the morning and brings them back in the evening. That is his life.

I used to work at a checkout in a grocery store. I was the guy who packed the bags as they came through. I am so old that I remember when they used to have paper bags at shops. You put the groceries in the bag for the shopper, and then someone would complain that you put the cold stuff in with the dry stuff or put this with that. I just did that all day, and it is kind of repetitive, isn't it? There are a lot of repetitive jobs out there. Now Moses is probably thinking, "I take care of sheep, so who am I that I could lead?"

Some scholars suggest that maybe there were three million Israelites in Egypt. Some scholars put it at a much smaller number.

Now think about it. You are driving home today, you see the bush on fire, and God says, "Hey!" How inadequate would you feel?

Moses probably thinks to himself, 'my mother gave me up at birth. I was raised among the people who aren't mine, I am a murderer, a runaway fugitive, and all I do all day is talk to sheep, and now you want me to go and see the fire, right? You want me to take all the Israelite people away, and they have been in captivity for so long they have forgotten their national identity. They have forgotten their customs. They have forgotten how to be together as a people.' So, Moses says to God, "God, you have got to be kidding. This is me."

Moses was allowing his history to affect his destiny. Moses let his past dominate what he could be in the future.

We know the story. Moses will lead them out of Egypt, and from them, he will form a people, and he will get them to the very edge of the Promised Land, and someone else will take them in.

CHAPTER FIVE

IT IS ALREADY IN YOU!

Moses would become a great leader, but something had to change for Moses to accomplish his destiny. But first, he had to discover that what he needed to achieve his destiny was already in him. It was already a part of him to be able to reach a better future.

Many of you need to realize that it is already in you. It is not necessarily something that you add. It is not something that will happen to you in the future. It has already happened to you. It is already in you.

Let me give you three ways to start strong when you're starting anything substantial, and these apply any time.

1. **<u>Your History is the platform for your Destiny</u>**
    Your history will give you strength for your future so that you can step into your destiny. Our past does not have to pilfer our success. We don't choose the family we are born into. We don't choose the place where we are born. Moses didn't select any of them, yet he was raised in a palace so that God could use him to lead a people out of Egypt and form a people one day. His mother pushed him down the Nile River to the princesses below, and God would save his life and raise him. His mother gave him away because God had a plan for his future and being given up was the doorway to achieving his destiny. Moses was raised in

the most powerful palace in the known world. He was in the footsteps of leadership and training and an environment where he could be prepared to be used by God to do something that no one had ever done.

It is probably why some scholars call him the most outstanding leader in human history. God was setting him up. His hurtful past would be what enabled him to become the person God called him to be.

Today, your past will open the door for your future. Those things that happened to you that you wish had never happened will open the door to your future. Those things that have happened to you that have been tremendously successful and joy-filled and caused you great happiness will also be used to open your future.

Once Moses stopped looking at his history as a burden, he was successful for his future.

Many of us look at our past and say, "I just wish it hadn't been that way," and we allow that to cripple our future.

Pharaoh directed the midwives to kill little boys, and even little Moses had to be thrown into the Nile. Yet, the Nile was the vehicle of execution that his mother would float him upon to a better life.

That which is meant for our destruction can be the very thing that raises us to life. The Nile, which was the vehicle of execution, became the exact vehicle through which he would achieve his success ultimately because he rode above that which could have destroyed him.

When we look at our past, we need to let go if we are to achieve. The very thing that we believe can kill us can destroy us and be the very thing that helps us accomplish the things that God wants us to accomplish in our lives.

There have been disappointments, hurts, let-downs, injustices, cruelties, and mistakes in all our lives. Have you ever considered your past, the wrong decisions that you made, errors you made as a parent? I have a heap of them myself. I am a dad of five kids, and there are so many things I wish I could have done better.

Now I can't change those circumstances. However, they can be the same things that allow me to achieve my destiny now. It is the same for you! Whether as a mom or a dad, in a friendship, sport, career, relationship, or unique purpose in your past.

In Luke 9:62,

> *Jesus said to him, "No one who puts a hand to the plow and looks back is fit for the kingdom of God." It is true that when they plowed behind the oxen, the guy who was plowing and holding looked into the distance at a spot, and as he went straight towards that spot, it would be in a straight line. But if he began to turn around and look backward, what will happen is the plow would go off to the side. So, when we look backward, it skews our future and robs our future.*

2. <u>**Recognize that you are not alone.**</u>
   - **We are not alone because God is with us,** and God makes a promise to us, *'I will never forsake you nor abandon you.'*

But also, God never forces you to respond to Him or move His way into your life. He will never pressurize you into His way of life.

I think that is why so many people have given up on church because the church at times has tried to force people to be a certain way, rather than allowing them to respond to an invitation that God gives to us.

- **We are not alone because we have allies.** We need people to strengthen us and keep our eyes on the future. We need people so that our histories become victories rather than our history become our burdens.

Can I ask you this question? Who have you got in your life who can help you be the man or woman that God wants you to be? Do you have someone? Do you know anybody? Moses says, "God, I can't speak." Later God supplies a man by Aaron, who is a speaker. God says, "Aaron will come and speak on your behalf." Do you ever feel inadequate and say, "I can't do that?" When Moses felt inadequate, God provided him with someone who could help him and strengthen him in his area of weakness.

Have you ever noticed that the person who stands behind you can make you capable? If you and I arm-wrestled, and then if someone else came alongside me and pressed their hand on top of my hand and pushed it down and gave strength to my hand, I would be a lot stronger. People coming alongside us in our lives can add power to us.

Often when we cannot do things by ourselves, we regress

into allowing our past to be the dictator of our destiny. Have you got an 'Aaron' in your life who can strengthen you?

3. **You must change.** That might sound obvious, but there are two things that you must change.

    -   **Change your attitude** by praying, talking to people, and reflecting on the role of your past. Your history does matter as it is what you stand on to achieve your future.

        I would prefer to decide to change my attitude than to make a resolution that I am not going to keep saying I am just going to give up ice cream, knowing that I will eat it fifteen minutes later.

    -   **Change your environment** by moving away from the situations, conversations, or circumstances and the people limiting what you can do.

So, how do you start strong?

I have learned that you have got to look forward from the point of view from this place of your history and life.

I have made many mistakes, and I also have a lot of good things in my history, but I have found that it is not the good things that have caused me to grow and be strong.

It has been my mistakes and the places where I have hurt people and myself that have robbed me and let me down. Yet they are the times that have truly made a difference in my life. There has been more growth from mistakes and hardship than the good or more accessible parts of my life.

Let us pray:

Lord God, I come before you right now, and I want to start this next season of my life strong. I do not want yesterday to deplete today. That does not mean the things that have happened to me, the cruelties done to me, the mistakes made are not true or don't have power. They do, but God, you are more capable than all of those. Lord, may I start this season by being able to say

- To that broken relationship that hurt me – 'You are behind me now.'

- To that mistake I made that hurt me and others – 'You are behind me now.'

- To the miscalculation I made that had all sorts of consequences. Can I say right now, 'You are behind me?'

- To those words, I spoke to someone I love that was so crushing – 'Now you have no power over me.'

- To those promises I have made that I have not kept. Can I say – 'You are behind me now?'

- To those opportunities that have been lost, can I tell them – 'You are behind me now?'

- To those cruel things that have been said to me that hurt me and caused me to cry caused me to question who I am. Can I tell them – 'You are behind me now?'

Lord God, I trust right now that I can start strong, and my future will be bright. I am here. My eyes are up. I am looking into the future. I am looking for opportunities to be the woman or the man I can be. I want my joy to increase. I want my happiness to increase. I want my peace to grow. I want my strength to rise. I want my victories to increase.

That does not mean I will not have troubles, problems, or difficulties, but I will have your strength as my foundation.

God, I pray that you would come and find me and be part of my life. Would you put people around me who will barrack for me, strengthen me, lend power to my arms so I can be the woman or man you want me to be?

God allows me to wrestle those attitudes in me that does not change in one action but change by establishing new habits, catching myself in the wrong attitude, and replacing it with the right attitude.

God, would you allow me to find environments that speak positively to me so that my future is bright?

God, I come before you for this season of Starting Strong, and I pray that it would be the best and most potent year or season that I have ever had in my life.

I can change none of yesterday, but I can change much of today if I am courageous and strong. God come to me, be magnificent, and, God, I am open, and I am prepared to do what I have never done before. Help me to be strong right now. In the name of Jesus, by the power of Your Holy Spirit. Amen.

CHAPTER SIX

THE DESTRUCTIVE POWER OF COMPROMISE

Can I ask you a question? Have you ever compromised on things that you believe in by the way you act or talk? I have, and the result is that it makes you feel annoyed and frustrated.

Another question, when you get close to achieving something, have you ever fallen into the trap of thinking near enough is good enough even though you know that near enough is not good enough? I have. Another question, have you ever known the right thing to do and just not done it? I have.

There are many reasons why.

I meet people who come to sit and talk with me, and I have done a fair bit of reading, and there are successful people who are cheating in life. Many of them will stop and will say, "I am not quite the person I want to be." I met someone recently who is tremendously wealthy and he said to me, 'I am just not the man that I want to be.'

We compromise for all sorts of different reasons, don't we? We compromise for obvious things like worrying about what people think. We make excuses like blaming the system you are working in for making life difficult, or that you were mistreated, or someone will get an advantage over me. Or we use that great term, 'It is just not fair.' There are so many reasons why we might compromise.

When we want to start something, we want to go back to the purest place of starting. So, therefore, you must address the compromise issue because the truth is in several areas of our lives, many of us are compromising.

We are compromising and compromise always robs us or leads us away from peacefulness.

One of the reasons we compromise is that it is so difficult to achieve what we want to do.

Together we will unfold a passage of Scripture from Numbers 20, verse 1. This passage is about Moses. After Jesus, scholars say that Moses was potentially the greatest leader in human history.

Moses was given the commandment by God to go and get the people out of Egypt. They were the workforce of Egypt at the time. As we know Moses initially questions, "Who am I? They are not going to listen to me. They are not going to come." Then God promises to take them from captivity to freedom.

However, Moses has got many challenges ahead of him:
1. He has got to believe in himself. We can all find that difficult at times.
2. He has got to be able to go and convince the Israelite people that God is saying it is time to move from captivity to freedom.

If you study groups of people, they can fall into ways of thinking and behaving when they're captured. We see it in society and around the world. It can happen on the micro-level and also have it on a large level. You see it within families where families begin to believe and think about themselves in a certain way, because of circumstances they are in, and they became captured. Then Moses has got to go and convince the Egyptians to let the Israelites go and rework their economy because they have been their slaves and done much of the hard work.

Eventually, Moses convinces them, but because the Israelites have been in captivity for 430 years, their sense of self-identity has been severely damaged. At that time, they were not allowed to be decision-makers. It says, they grumble the whole time they are being led from captivity all the way to freedom.

If any of you are parents, have you ever had a child who is stuck in a way of thinking or feeling emotional, and you know that to get free from the captivity they are in and bring to a place of maturity and freedom, that there are going to be some decisions that must be made? Sometimes they are complex, and the kids got to go through it, yet they keep just wanting to come back to you to make things easier for them.

CHAPTER SEVEN

CAPTURED BY CIRCUMSTANCES

The grumbling people being led by Moses from captivity to freedom run out of water and turn against him. We are going to read from Numbers 20, verse 1-4:

> *In the first month, the whole Israelite community arrived at the Desert of Zin, and they stayed at Kadesh. There Miriam died and was buried. Now there was no water for the community, and the people gathered in opposition to Moses and Aaron. They quarreled with Moses and said, "If only we had died when our brothers fell dead before the Lord! Why did you bring the Lord's community into this wilderness, that we and our livestock should die here?"*

They are traveling from one place to another. God has promised to get them out of captivity and that He will take them to the Promised Land. God has promised that He will look after them, that God will get them there. Then suddenly, they ran out of water, and they immediately begin to complain and grumble.

The other version of this story in Exodus says that they turned on Moses and wanted to stone him to death. They wanted to kill the very person who was leading them from captivity to freedom just because they had run out of water.

The people had taken their eyes off the promise that God had given them because of their current circumstances.

We often do the same thing. We get married, we start a new job, we start a family, we make some decisions about how we are going to live and what we are going to do. We have a dream and a vision of what we are meant to be and then suddenly, for various reasons, circumstances, difficulties, and failures and our human frailty come along.

What happens is we take our eyes off the vision of what we want to be, and we look at the circumstances of what is happening. Then to live at that lesser level, we begin to compromise on things along the way. In verse 2 it says:

> *There was no water for the congregation. So, they gathered against Moses and Aaron. They quarreled with Moses and said, "If only we had died when our brothers fell dead before the Lord!" And then they say, 'Why did you bring the Lord's community into this wilderness, that we and our livestock should die here?'*

Why did you bring us here? Some people complained and in the other versions of this story say, "Why didn't you just leave us captive?"

They were captive in their thoughts. We can be too. They were captive in their lives. We can be too. They were captive to their circumstances. We can be too.

> *We can be stuck because of what we were born into and because our parents live in certain ways just like the Israelites. But Moses is trying to take them from*

captivity to freedom and here they run out of water
and now are just going to die.

You can hear it in them that they had become comfortable with being captive. With captivity, they survived so they ask Moses why he brought them out of Egypt to such a wretched place. The place had no grain, figs, vines, or pomegranates, and there was no water to drink. The people are looking hard at their circumstances, aren't they?

Moses and Aaron went from the assembly to the entrance to the tent of meeting and fell facedown, and the glory of the Lord appeared to them. The Lord said to Moses, "Take the staff, and you and your brother Aaron gather the assembly together. Speak to that rock before their eyes and it will pour out its water. You will bring water out of the rock for the community so they and their livestock can drink.

The people complain. It is a bit like hearing people come and complain to me about things, and I listen to them and wonder what I am going to do. And sometimes I go to God and say, 'God, I need some wisdom. Tell me how to deal with this.'

People complain and Moses probably thinks, 'I cannot do any better. I am pouring my life out here. I put my career on hold. My income is gone. You are not looking at me. I am just leading you. Look what I am doing for you. And you are just a bunch of complainers. I have got no more to give any of you.' Have you ever been there where you feel as if you are doing everything you can and yet your plans are not coming together?

CHAPTER EIGHT

CAPTURED BY DISOBEDIENCE

M oses went to God, and then he and Aaron went away from the assembly to the entrance of the tent, the place where they came before God to worship God.

...and fell facedown, and the glory of the Lord appeared to them.

The Lord said to Moses, "Take the staff, and you and your brother Aaron gather the assembly together. Speak to that rock before their eyes and it will pour out its water.

God says I want you to go up to that rock and say to the rock, 'give water.'

You will bring water out of the rock for the community so they and their livestock can drink.

It is interesting how people in leadership, whether you are leading in your workplace, your family, or in a ministry in the church, are often required to do unreasonable things that followers do not understand.

So, Moses took the staff from the Lord's presence, just as he commanded him. He and Aaron gathered the assembly together in front of the rock and Moses said to them, "Listen, you rebels, must we bring you water out of this rock?" Then Moses raised his arm and struck the rock twice with his staff. Water gushed out, and the community and their livestock drank.

But what happens to Moses and Aaron because of that?

But the Lord said to Moses and Aaron, "Because you did not trust in me enough to honor me as holy in the sight of the Israelites, you will not bring this community into the land I give them."

God says to Aaron and Moses, "You did not trust that I would be holy and you did not trust that I would fulfill my promise. You did not do what I told you to do and because of that, you will not enter the Promised Land."

The people grumbled and it is the job of leadership to respond, but to respond in the right and appropriate way. Unfortunately, Moses and Aaron responded wrongly, and as leaders, they paid the price along with the people. Let me explain. Why did Moses and Aaron not get to the Promised Land? God told them what to do and they did not do it.

Verse 11 says:

Then Moses raised his arm and struck the rock twice with his staff.

But God did not say that. It said earlier in verse 8:

*Take the staff, and you and your brother Aaron gather
the assembly together. Speak to that rock before their
eyes and it will pour out its water.*

But they did not command the rock. They did not speak to the rock.
They hit the rock and commentators and theologians tell us that God
had commanded them to speak to the rock and say bring forth water,
but they said,

*"Listen, you rebels, must we bring you water out of
this rock?"*

Moses got the staff and out of frustration, said, "You rebels" and hit
the rock in frustration.

There are some of you right now who know the right thing to do
in your heart about things in your life and you are doing something that is kind of close, but it is not exactly what you are meant
to do.

'Close' does not get us all that God wants for us.

'Close' does not get us all the way.

Theologians say the other reason that they did not get into the
Promised Land was they asked, *"Shall we bring the water out?"* In
doing this, they take credit for something that they could not do.
Moses said, *"Do you want me to get the water out? Should I get it?"*
They turn it upon themselves.

And my point is simply this – in our lives, sometimes we know the
right thing to do, and we think that close enough is good enough. But

unfortunately, that attitude sells us and everyone around us short.

Let me give you a couple of examples. Someone might say, "I take paint, pens and paper, and stationery from where I work. It is not money or the big stuff." Someone might say, "I come home from work to be with my family but don't expect me to spend time and talk with them. I am home and that is near enough."

It is "I studied to pass the exams but not learn the content." That was me. When I buy presents for my wife, I just buy chocolate because it is much easier than going through the effort of going to the shops and walking around for hours and finding something. Whenever I go to the shops, even though there are 250 shops, there is nothing there to buy. A married man might say, "I look at other women and I wish my wife looked like that, but I do not touch. I'm near enough, but I'm not close enough." Or "I talk about other women with my girlfriends. I just don't tell her. I hope they don't talk about me like that." People say I wanted to be, I wanted to go, I wanted to do, but it is just easier not to.

When we start strong, near enough is not good enough, but it will get us by. So we end up starting out, then we stop, and we say, "I am not the person I really want to be," but we didn't seek completely after doing the right thing.

God speaks to us about our jobs, the relationships we are in, the friendships we have, the people that we are married to, and that we love. God speaks to us about those things, about the children we have or the houses or the investments and the way we spend our money, the way we rest, the way we go on holidays. These are all things that God speaks to us about because He is involved in all the aspects of our lives.

Do you want to do what God has placed on your heart or do you want to just get close enough and be a good person?

CHAPTER NINE

BEYOND REPROACH

There are certain behaviors that we would call unacceptable in our lives, right? There are things like murder that are obviously unacceptable. I think it is unacceptable that men and women who do the same job, don't get paid the same amount of money. I think it is unacceptable that there are many women who are great leaders but don't get the opportunity to lead and there is a whole pile of other things in society that are just unacceptable.

There are behaviors that society says are acceptable, that is, that you are allowed to do. They are acceptable by world standards. They are acceptable, but there is another standard when we come to God's way. And the other standard is what is called 'beyond reproach,' in the Scriptures.

Often when I am thinking about what I can or cannot do, I think what would be acceptable. This will be okay. For many of us, we live our lives, thinking, 'I am a good person because I am living here at this acceptable level.' But as Christian people, God calls us and asks us to live up here at this higher level or way called 'beyond reproach.' What does reproach mean?

Reproach means 'criticize adversely, or reprimand or blame or accusation.' We are called to live in a place where no accusation can be brought against us. We are called to live in a place with no blind spot where we cannot be censured. It means not deciding that a certain lower way of living is okay and acceptable. For example, I have regularly met men who have said to me, "Listen, I would love my wife to look like that. So, I just looked, but I didn't touch. See? And I have said to myself this is quite acceptable."

It really is an acceptable behavior, but it robs them and their relationship of who they can be because that is not God's way. One time when I had spoken at a breakfast, a business guy came to me afterward and said, "Are you suggesting that I run my business according to Christian principles and be a Christian in the marketplace?" And I said, "Yes." He said, "I would get killed. I could not compete in the marketplace. I would go broke if I ran my business as a Christian." Then he said, "I just decided to live at this level knowing that I am not really living according to my values."

Many of us do that, don't we? So many of us have dreams about who we want to be, but we accept something less than what we could be. And maybe you have been thinking to yourself, 'I am going to start something. I am going to do something. I am going to …'

This is an opportunity to start afresh, but unless you address the issue of doing what is on your heart and remember that *"to strike the rock two times"* is not what God said. He said, *"Speak to it."*

Where in your life do you know that you are meant to be living, doing, acting, believing, and serving in your life? You know you are saying, "I am just close enough." But, at the end of the day, years down the track, you will stop and remember, "I am not fully the man or woman I want to be because along the way, I lived fractionally less than I wanted to be. I was not someone 'beyond reproach.' I was someone who was acceptable by the world."

Christians often say, "This is it. We will just go to this level," but do not stop and say, "What is God asking of me?"

Some people say, "It is so hard to live at that higher level." But there is a secret to living beyond reproach and it is called trust in God. Trusting that this is where God has called me to live. He has called me to live in keeping with His word. He has spoken to me and given me conviction about my marriage, about my business, about the way I spend my money, the way I invest, or where I live.

Many of us have settled for places at times in our lives. I know I have settled for knowing the right thing to do and just not doing it or feeling like close enough is good enough. It robs us of a sense of peace, joy, and happiness and it depletes our retirement; and robs our marriages and our friendships. It diminishes the way we are mums and dads because when we stop and say, "This is who I want to be up here, but what I choose is just acceptable."

Today, are you doing everything in your heart to say, 'I am in the right place with where I am meant to be?'

Surely if we are talking about starting strong, you go back to the beginning. You don't want to start already behind.

How do we stay strong? It is not just good enough to start if you start something well and then you peter out. Some of us compromise on our convictions because we made a past mistake that we cannot change. We see it in ourselves, in our families, in our work and it affects every part of us, and we think, "I cannot come back from that." But that is just not true.

Some of us have let someone down and so, we live at this level with an acceptable life, but we do not live at the higher area where no one could turn around and say, you are not living 'everything.' You can be someone who says, "We did not get the money that we needed," or "We did not get chosen," or "Our child is just difficult to talk with, and so, we have made the decision not to even try. We were frightened of failing and so, we live less than we are meant to be." Wouldn't it be great to be able to walk around and say, "I am in my life where God has called me to be right now?"

At the beginning of this season, wouldn't it be good to say, "I am just going to take a little stock take? Then I am going to go back and do a bit of homework." I often figuratively take myself away somewhere, sit, and journal. I journal my praise and ask, is this where I want to be? Because I don't need to be less. God has asked me to run 100% purely, not 95%.

CHAPTER TEN

DOING WHAT GOD SAYS

heard a reading at Mass recently that really spoke to me. I remember studying theology at university and spending a lot of time on this passage of Scripture in John 2, verse 1.

I'm just going to make one point:

> *On the third day, a wedding took place at Cana in Galilee. Jesus' mother was there, and Jesus and his disciples had also been invited to the wedding. When the wine was gone, Jesus' mother said to him, "They have no more wine." "Woman, why do you involve me?" Jesus replied. "My hour has not yet come." His mother said to the servants, "Do whatever he tells you.*

Here is Jesus, and He is probably about thirty years of age. He has not started His public ministry yet. This is His first outing with His mother, and they go to a wedding, His mother turns to Him and says, "They have run out of wine." Jewish weddings went for seven days! Imagine a wedding that goes for seven days and at this wedding, they ran out of alcohol. Rosemary says to me from time to time that women are more observant than men. Do you think that is true? Well, that may be true, but I reckon that most men would have realized they had run out of booze!

Mary, says to Jesus "They have run out of wine," and we read the story from verse 4:

> *"Woman, what concern is that to you and to me?"*
> *Jesus replied. "My hour has not yet come." His mother*
> *said to the servants, "Do whatever he tells you."*
> *Nearby stood six stone water jars, the kind used by*
> *the Jews for ceremonial washing, each holding from*
> *twenty to thirty gallons.*
>
> *Jesus said to the servants, "Fill the jars with water"*
> *so, they filled them to the brim.*
>
> *He said to them, "Now draw some out, and take it to*
> *the chief steward." So they took it. When the steward*
> *tasted the water that had become wine and did not*
> *know where it came from (though the servants who*
> *had drawn the water knew), the steward called the*
> *bridegroom and said to him, "Everyone serves the*
> *good wine first, and then the inferior wine after the*
> *guests have become drunk. But you have kept the*
> *good wine until now."*

The priest who read this at Mass commented that this Scripture is about us doing what God says. I thought, wow, that is just too simple but so true.

What has God said to you about your marriage?

What has God said to you about where you are today?

You cannot change yesterday. So, we have got to go forward from where we are.

God is the one who gives us the opportunity to start again.

Some of us are very successful in our work, lives, and what we have done and achieved in sport and media and the sciences, and the arts.

But if you scratch the surface, we stop and say, I am not everything.

I am too scared to be everything I can be because there is a risk involved. So, I would prefer just to live in captivity and be less than what I can be.

That is not how you start. You can't begin strong when you are already behind.

This priest was saying what Mary was saying of Jesus, *'Just do what He says.'*

That is the answer. It is simple. What would happen if you made the decision to just ask the question, 'What do I need to do to be able to say I'm 100%? What do I need to do to deal with those feelings of disappointment from my past, the places I have been let down, the places I have been hurt? What do I need to do? '

That is the secret. It is coming to God and saying, "God, you need to do it in me to start strong."

Many years ago, I was living in Brisbane, which is up north on the east coast of Australia, and I travelled to live in Perth, in Western Australia, which is 3000 kilometers away or around two and a half thousand miles.

I had moved to Brisbane and got married a couple of years earlier. When I moved back to Perth, I realized everybody I had known previously didn't know me anymore. In Brisbane, everybody knew me and so, everybody treated me in a certain way. They said, "Oh, it's Bruce." But when I moved to the other side of the country, I didn't know anybody anymore. It occurred to me one day and I felt like God whispered in my ear, "Be the person you have always wanted to be, and not the person everybody allows you to be. Come back to that dream that God put in you that you have allowed circumstances to knock out of you."

I have worked with a lot of young people over the years. I used to often say to young people and adults too, when you meet people for the first time and you know that you are possibly going to have a bit of a future, "I know I do not know you, but we are obviously going to get to know each other. How you act toward me is how I will act back to you. You set the tone. So, if you want to come in shy, or you want to come in hurting or limping into this relationship, I will have to treat you the same way. That is how I am going to relate to you. But if you come in as the person you want to be, I am going to treat you like that because I will not know any different."

I had always dreamed of giving talks and I remember being thirty years old and I had never given a talk in public in my life, but I had believed that from the time I had been in school. Many nights for 10 or 12 years, I would get in the shower, and I would put the showerhead at the right level, and I would give a talk in the shower. I did that for years and then one night, I was at an event, and someone asked me to give a talk and I had about an hour to prepare. I had never given a talk in my whole life, and I remember I walked away, and I heard this voice, God, say to me, "Be who you are in the shower. They don't know you any other way."

As we join or come to churches, come into places of work, come into new places, I encourage you to be the woman or man you want to be and not the person that others allow you to be, or you've allowed yourself to be.

How do you become that? By doing what God has asked you to do precisely.

Moses and Aaron hit the rock a couple of times and did not command the rock.

It is not that much different, is it, really? They were still addressing the rock but those little compromises that take us away from the very thing that we're meant to do often have such a devastating impact upon us. Being less robs us of a sense of peace and being able to say I am in the place that I'm meant to be.

This is the message of Jesus.

CHAPTER ELEVEN

TRUST IN GOD

B lessed are those who trust in the Lord, whose trust is the Lord. They shall be like a tree planted by water, sending out its roots by the stream. It shall not fear when heat comes, and its leaves shall stay green; in the year of drought, it is not anxious, and it does not cease to bear fruit. (Jeremiah 17: 7 – 8)

'It is not anxious, and it does not cease to bear fruit.' This beautiful passage of Scripture starts by saying, 'Blessed are those whose trust is the Lord.' as you start this next season I encourage you to trust God, trust God for your life, trust God for your family, trust God for your circumstance and trust God for your direction.

The Scripture asks, "Whose trust is in the Lord?" So, we stop and say, "God, I trust you. I commit my life and my plans over to you. I trust you. Come and be with me, Lord, as I'm trusting you."

What happens if you trust? It says in Jeremiah,

'They shall be like a tree planted by water.'

Trees need water, so that makes sense.

'Sending out its roots by the stream,'

Meaning it has water all the time because the roots are by the stream. It is the same with our relationship with God. As we trust God, standing close to God, we shall not fear. *'When the heat comes, its leaves shall stay green.'* Why? Because it is rooted in the presence of God, and it's right there drinking from the presence of God.

'Even when drought comes' and it is anxious, as it says in the Scripture, *'it is not anxious, and it does not cease to bear fruit.'* On the contrary, it can bear fruit all the time. Why? Because it is right beside the stream.

As we go this next season, trust God with your life.

Trust God with your direction.

Trust God that He has a good plan for you.

Trust God that He wants to see you blessed.

Trust God that He wants to see things go well in life.

Trust God that when drought and difficulty come, He will get you to the other side.

In other words, we keep saying, "God, in you I trust. My eyes are set upon you. My eyes are not to the left or the right." We can talk about things like Jesus and the Holy Spirit, and we can talk about all those theological and doctrinal things, and they are tremendously important to talk about. But this is a time when we are looking at ourselves and turning our heart towards God and saying to you,

Jesus, we say to you, Holy Spirit, we say to you, God, the Father, "I am trusting in you." It is a prayer of surrender to God.

This is not talking about God, but this is our heart and spirit talking to God and encountering Jesus in our life, through the power of the Holy Spirit, where we will know the love of the Father.

I encourage you not to fear as we start this next season. Trust God. He is going to look after you. Trust Him. You are going to have a great year. Trust Him that even though you may face some difficulty, you are going to get to the other side. You can trust that God is with you. Each day, say, "I am trusting you, Lord." Blessed are those who trust in the Lord.

CHAPTER TWELVE

STAND FIRM

I want to help you in your prayer today by sharing something with you that has really helped me. So, I'm going to go back into the Old Testament. We know the story of the chosen people crossing over the Red Sea when the Red Sea parted. They went through the parted sea and the Egyptian army who was coming behind them to attack them was ultimately consumed by the sea.

God asks us to go in a particular direction and to do a specific thing and to live in a certain way and to have a certain mindset and a certain peacefulness.

We know that in life, we will have struggles. There will be times when all of that will work out fantastically, but then there will be times when we will have challenges and difficulties. In those times of challenge, the Scriptures give us an indication of what we are meant to do right there.

I encourage you to read Exodus 14 to help you approach this next season or year in prayer and particularly the challenges you will have. A quick summary: the Hebrew people are on the edge of the Red Sea, and they are about to cross, but the Egyptian Pharaoh, the king, and the leaders of Egypt realized they had done the wrong thing by letting the Hebrew people go from the captivity that they've been under for 430 years, so they send the army to get them. The people of Israel look up and suddenly see the Egyptian army coming to get them. They have got the army on one side of them and the Red Sea on the other. So, they turn to Moses, and they begin to panic. We can all panic when we see challenges, can't we? Moses gives them an indication of how we are meant to live, and I have found this very powerful and very true in my life.

Beginning with Exodus 14:10, it says:

> As Pharaoh drew near, the Israelites looked back, and there were the Egyptians advancing on them. In great fear, the Israelites cried out to the Lord. They said to Moses, "Was it because there were no graves in Egypt that you have taken us away to die in the wilderness?"

The people panic. They think they could have just stayed in Egypt and died. Because the people didn't want to leave captivity, they ask Moses, "What have you done to us bringing us out of Egypt? Is this not the very thing we told you in Egypt? Let us alone and let us serve the Egyptians."

They had become accustomed to being captive to the Egyptians, but Moses wanted to set them free. They said, "It would have been better for us to serve the Egyptians than to die here in the wilderness."

But Moses said to the people, 'Do not be afraid, stand firm.'

Stand firm on how God is leading you. Stand firm in the place where you are. Do not be afraid. Stand firm and see the deliverance that the Lord will accomplish for you today.

So, Moses is telling them not to panic.

> *"Do not be afraid, stand firm, and see the deliverance*
> *that the Lord will accomplish for you today; for the*
> *Egyptians whom you see today you shall never see*
> *again."*

Moses reminds the people if they stand firm, they will never see the problem they see today again.

I strongly encourage you to write verse 14 on a card, keep it in your pocket or on your fridge, or right where you get ready in the morning: The Lord will fight for you, and you have only to keep still.

So, Moses assured them that even though the Egyptians were coming to get them and the problem was serious, they must stand firm and the Lord would fight for them if they only keep still.

There are times when our businesses are struggling or when relationships can be difficult. These are the times to stand firm in the truth. As it says, the Lord will fight for you. The Lord must do it.

As a ministry where we are right now, the Coronavirus has absolutely smashed us from a support point of view. The fact that we get through is up to God. He must fight for us. There's nothing more we can do.

We just need to stand firm. We need to stop and not panic. We need to remain at peace and God will fight for us. That is true for so many of us in so many ways in our lives.

It is true for you in things that you will face this season or year. So, how do you stand firm? You stand firm by being a person who is regularly in prayer every day, talking to God, listening to God, and continually saying to God, "God, I love you with my whole heart, soul, mind, and strength."

In the New Testament, Jesus says, *'Don't worry.'* It is very challenging to stand firm when facing difficulties, but that is when we can pray. We can consistently come before God and ask Him to be with us.

In other words, Jesus is either the Lord of your life or He is not.

If you are in the right place and say, "God, I commit my life to you." If you learn to stand firm, it is amazing how strong you will become in your walk with God and how strong you become as a person in your marriage, in your relationships, in your business, and being able to walk into your future. It is an amazing principle of the Scripture. It is so powerful. Stand firm. Don't panic.

I am speaking this and declaring this message to me as much as I am to anybody else. I tell my children this. I tell the people that I love the most in my life this, "Stand firm, and don't panic." If you have given your life to God, He will fight for you.

CHAPTER THIRTEEN

STILLNESS

Am I the person that God has called me to be? Am I the person that I am meant to be is how most people say it. Am I happy in the place that God has called me to be?

We understand stillness is 'being' in the sense of being still, doing nothing as in inactivity, but when we read the Bible, stillness is meant to be something active.

Can you picture Moses and the Israelites when right in front of them is the Red Sea but right behind them is the Egyptian army and they are hemmed in. Yet they have a promise from God that God will take them to a promised land and that God has got a future for them.

The Hebrew people only left Egypt because Moses declared God's promise of who they were to them. That is all they have to hold onto.

Their circumstances are that in front of them, they have the Red Sea, and behind them, they have the Egyptian army who is going to capture or kill them. So, what do they do?

Moses looks at the Hebrew people as they begin to panic and ask, "Why did we leave Egypt? We should have stayed in Egypt." Then in Exodus 14, Moses looked at them and said:

"The Lord will fight for you, and you have only to keep still."

What does that mean?

When I was about nine years old, Mum and Dad took me to the dentist, and I had to have a tooth pulled out. The dentist gave me an anesthetic, waited for a while, and then said to me, "Does it feel numb now?" I did not know what numb felt like, so I said, "Yes." I still vividly remember the dentist saying, "Open your mouth," and he held up his bright silver pliers, put them on the tooth and he pulled the tooth out. As he pulled the tooth, the anesthetic had not fully worked, and it immediately burst into pain. It was extraordinary pain and there was blood everywhere. I was so scared and that feeling of 'scared' would grow into tangible fear in the years to come.

It is a vivid memory. I was nine years old, and I can tell you exactly where I was and what it was like. That fear caused me to be terrified of dentists, which many of us are, but I was super frightened after that bad experience.

Consequently, I did not go to the dentist very often. Last year I had to have a filling and I have never had my teeth drilled or had a filling since that earlier experience. The dentists have never said that I needed to, but, to be honest, I have not been to many dentists. I turned up for my appointment and I was petrified.

There was a young dentist who was only old enough to be one of my children and a young dental nurse and I was in the room alone with them. They told me to get on the chair and they pressed the button, so the chair moved back. The dentist says, "Open up," and then he lifts the shiny drill towards me. At that point in time, I had to keep pushing down the fear. I had to actively 'be still,' push down the fear and control myself.

I repeated in my head, "Do not panic, do not panic, do not panic," and I had to actively work at making sure that I overcame the fear rising within me.

Here are the Hebrew people. They have got the Red Sea in front of them, and they have got an army behind them saying, "We are going to capture you and kill you." Moses is saying, "Be still, and hold down the fear. The Lord will fight for you." In other words, "Remember the promise of what God is going to do for you."

What does that mean for you and me in our lives?

You and I are called to be in a relationship with God, to encounter God, to hear God's voice in our life, and for God to be active within our lives.

We can connect with God through prayer, spiritual reading, and listening to the teaching of the church. We come before God and we come to that sense of, 'This is what God is saying to me.' We hold on to the promise.

What Moses is saying to them is, "The Lord will fight for you. You have only to stand still." In other words, work at being confident in God. It is an action. It is not just being still.

Being confident in God is 'work.' As you come into this new season or year, what might God say to you? What is God saying to you?

What is the direction or the trajectory of your life right now?

You might say I am retired and I am not working. That means you can be more deeply in a personal relationship with God. Maybe you are someone who is young and just starting out and you have got a whole number of things that you want to do. That means you can walk more deeply in God to hold the promise.

Maybe you are right in the middle of your work, your career, raising children, perhaps you're waiting, maybe you are separated and going through a divorce, or you are just still in the place where you have always been. Maybe you are someone who has lost your job. You have just got to stand in the place where you are and even though there is opposition behind you, and it looks like there are no doors open in front of you, have confidence in God.

God fights for us. He could open pathways for you.

God parts the Red Sea for the Hebrew people to go through and ultimately, the sea would close over the Egyptian army, and be defeated.

Find a piece of paper and write down who you see yourself being in twelve months from now. Hold onto that and have confidence that God is talking to you as that comes out of your prayer. I think you can take some time and stand still, but remember, stillness is not the same as doing nothing.

Stillness is being very actively engaged. That is why prayer is so important. I am not trying to teach you anything. I am not trying to inspire you. I am trying to bring you to a place where you could pray and you would hear the voice of God because if you hear God,

He will transform your life.

How do we hear God?

We hear God when we pray.

CHAPTER FOURTEEN

DEVELOP EYES TO SEE

One of the spiritual disciplines that we need to develop in our life is the ability to see what God has done in our lives. We see that by looking back. We see that in our prayer when we reflect upon the things we are going through. So, we are constantly aware that we are in a relationship with God.

Rosemary and I have been married for many years and we can look back to our times before we had children, those times when we had our children, when they were very little and they went through primary school or grade school, then they went into high school. Then they went off to college and university. They have all grown, left home, and some have their own children. So, we went through all those phases, and we can look back and see the good and the not-so-good that happened throughout our lives.

It is the same in our relationship with God. We must look back because looking back gives us confidence for the future.

The Scriptures tell us that faith increases and grows. It becomes more in us. As you know, this ministry is unique because we are trying to proclaim the gospel in ways that people who do not go to church or people who are really looking for extra growth in their life can find it. One of the significant challenges for us has always been the financial aspect. We have to walk in faith as we wonder if we will ever survive.

Some time ago, I sat my staff down. We were running out of money, and it was evident, and I said to all of them, "We are going to keep going. We are not going to stop. We are going to trust that God will somehow get us through this." Sure enough, we got through.

Somehow, we survived. A year or two goes by. Then suddenly, through various circumstances, we face the same issue, and we are running out of money again. So, I gathered all the staff from younger people who have got young families to older people and everything in between. I sat them down in fairness and said to them, "It looks like we are going to run out of money, and I do not know what we can do. So, I am saying to all of you, if you need to leave because you need to go and find security, then do that." I remember one young woman who was about 30 years old and the mother of four children said to me, "God got us through last time when we were facing oblivion on every side and God will come through again." She started crying and she said, "I will not give up because God is faithful. He looked after us last time and He will look after us again." And she said, "I will not go anywhere else." Sure enough, she was right, and God did look after us. But how did she come to that place?

God is so active in your life and yet, sometimes, we do not see that because we do not pray. Pray through the hardship of our marriages, the struggles we faced financially, the times when we have looked at our jobs and been unfulfilled or when there have been successes that have come in our marriages, work, or our other circumstances. By looking back, we begin to develop the eyes to see spiritually and that has an amazing effect on our future.

Look at Exodus 14, verse 13:

> *But Moses said to the people, "Do not be afraid,*
> *stand firm, and see the deliverance that the Lord*
> *will accomplish for you today; for the Egyptians*
> *whom you see today you shall never see again.*

Moses tells the people that the objection that they have got in front of them is gone and they will see the deliverance that the Lord will accomplish for them. In other words, see what God is going to do. God is going to lift you out of the circumstance that you face now.

I have been around for a while, and new seasons and 31st December keep turning up. God is inviting us into a relationship of depth where we see Him, and we know Him and He is part of our life in a more profound way.

If today, you are nineteen years old and you hear that God has got more for you, it can be deeper. It is so true.

If you are eighty-nine years old today and you are reading, I want to say to you, God has got so much more, but we must open our eyes to see.

Today, in your prayer, look back and see how God has been a part of your life. Develop the ability to see God in your life.

> *Moses said to the people, "Do not be afraid, stand*
> *firm, and see the deliverance that the Lord will*
> *accomplish for you today.*

That young woman who looked at me in tears and said, "God will not let us down," doesn't mean it wasn't difficult. But we can have confidence that God will not let us down because He was faithful in the past and He will be faithful again. We had learned to see what would happen and you can be the same if you learn to see where God has worked in your past.

CHAPTER FIFTEEN

JESUS IN THE ORDINARY

t may be the beginning of the year or a new season, or you are making a new start and it matters how you move forward. How we start this season will largely dictate how this year will go and all we will achieve in becoming the people God has called us to be.

Most people do not walk around saying, 'I am trying to be the person God calls me to be.' I realize that is a God language, but at the end of the day, we were put on the planet by God to be the person He calls us to be in our own personal life and in the practical things of life and in our spiritual life.

There are things that we need to grow in, but the truth is they are very much connected. You cannot be falling apart in one area of your life. You are living in ways that you should not be living. You are not doing the things you're meant to be doing, yet you turn up to church and pray the whole time. You have your prayer time during the day, but you are not living the right way in your life.

It does not mean that we do not have faults, we do, but the truth is our spiritual life is the totality of everything that we are. As we tune into God for the things that we want to achieve in terms of our relationships, our work, the kind of person we are, that is all deeply linked to our spirituality and being able to see God in our lives.

We read in Luke's gospel, in chapter 8, verse 22, a passage where the apostle's eyes are opened.

> One day he got into a boat with his disciples, and he said to them, "Let us go across to the other side of the lake." So, they put out, and while they were sailing, he fell asleep. A windstorm swept down on the lake, and the boat was filling with water, and they were in danger.
>
> They went to him and woke him up, shouting, "Master, Master, we are perishing!" And he woke up and rebuked the wind and the raging waves; they ceased, and there was a calm. He said to them, "Where is your faith?" They were afraid and amazed, and said to one another, "Who then is this, that he commands even the winds and the water, and they obey him?"

I love this passage of Scripture because what we see in the apostles, these disciples, these followers of His is this continuing understanding and revelation of who God is in their life as they are doing the ordinary things of life. Here they are just in a boat crossing a lake in that part of the world, which was normal for them to do. They were having a spiritual moment and it was not at church. It was not that they were having their prayer time as such, no. They were just doing the ordinary things of their life.

Jesus comes and Jesus works miraculously.

It is the same for you and me. In the ordinariness of everyday life, we have a routine to our life of when we get up and do certain things, and we go out to certain places. This is true whether we are someone who is retired, whether we are someone who is actively at work, or whether we are a student, there is a routine in our lives.

And it is into that routine that Jesus comes.

It is into that routine that we need to develop the eyesight to see Jesus in our life.

Jesus seeks to be in the ordinary, but we must try to see just as we discussed Moses earlier, saying to the Hebrew people, *"See how God will deliver you."* We must choose to see.

The seeing and the increasing ability to see develops by a commitment of our attitude. It grows by the regular habit of prayer or talking to God.

I want to encourage you today. I have written books or collected prayers written by lots of beautiful people, the saints, the Popes, holy men, and women through history and prayers that really have spoken to me. I say those prayers because sometimes they really capture the things I want to say.

I have also learned because it was drummed into me by a Catholic priest and by priests and other religious people I look up to about talking to God and being in this intimate relationship where I am talking to God as if I am talking while I am talking to you right now, I am just talking to a friend. So, this focus on a relationship conversation with God is tremendously important.

It is about bringing the totality of ourselves to God. I want to encourage you to have your time of daily prayer. I pray according to the PERSONAL method of prayer, where the R in the acronym 'personal' stands for Real. I write all kinds of experiences in my prayer journal and God sees me as being real in my life today. I ask God, "May I be able to hear your voice all around me, walking with me and talking with me and being in my life." And so, Jesus is going to come to us in the everyday happenings of our life.

In this case, the disciples got frightened, but Jesus comes to us in joy. Jesus comes to us in the fun and the marvelous things that are happening.

We must learn to see, and not necessarily with our eyes, but see with the eyes of our heart. It is an ability to choose the presence of God and see God in our life. It comes in prayer, and it comes as a sense that we carry around us all the time.

Wherever you are today, have the sense that God is with you and develop the ability to see. It will come. Suddenly it will come into view. You begin to be able to see God's presence and experience God's presence around you. And if you can see, it is amazing how you begin to see the future and a sense of peace and calm descends upon you in your life.

As you open yourself to the power of God, which is the Holy Spirit alive today, why don't you decide to begin to see God in the ordinary?

CHAPTER SIXTEEN

SIT WITH GOD

Mary is someone in the Scriptures who 'sees.' If we go right back to when Jesus was born and the angels and the shepherds and the magi come and visit, we read a fascinating verse of Scripture about Mary. I want to reflect on this because there is so much we can learn from it.

In Luke 2:15-19, it says:

> When the angels had left them and gone into the heavens, the shepherd said to one another, because the angels had appeared to the shepherds and told them what was happening. Let us go now to Bethlehem and see this thing that has taken place, which the Lord has made known to us. So, they went with haste and found Mary and Joseph and the child lying in the manger. When they saw this, they made known what had been told them about this child who told them the angels and all who heard it were amazed at what the shepherds told them. But Mary treasured all these words and pondered them in her heart. But Mary treasured all these words and pondered them in her heart. But Mary treasured all these words and pondered them in her heart.

Mary heard what the shepherds had said that the angels had told them. Mary listens to all of this. Mary is the one that the angel Gabriel had appeared to and said, *"You are going to be the mother of the Lord, even though you know not man."* Mary is a young teenage girl having a baby in a place alone, with just her husband, Joseph.

What do we see Mary do? It says,

> *"Mary treasured all these things and pondered them in her heart."*

In other words, Mary took all these things in that were happening around her and then *'she pondered them.'* What does this mean? Mary sat with them and *'pondered,'* which means maybe she didn't understand it all at first. Pondered means she did not fully comprehend all aspects of it.

Mary probably understood some of it, but she let it sit with her, not knowing fully all that would happen in the future and all that it meant in our relationship with God.

If we were truthful, we do not know everything and I am not talking about academics. I think one of the Catholic church's problems and its beautiful richness is that there is so much knowledge to be had.

The problem with that is that because there is so much knowledge, we sometimes feel disempowered because we do not know enough.

We say, "The priest knows, or that religious person knows," and we dismiss it, even diminishing and reducing our relationship with God because there is always more knowledge to be had.

There is a sadness that many people do not have a rich relationship with God because they sense they do not know enough. But our relationship with God is meant to be a personal relationship with God where God reveals truth to us, where God speaks, and we encounter God in our life.

Pondering is a way of ultimately coming to see by just 'sitting.'

Years ago, the priest who taught me to pray would say, "Just sit, Bruce, just sit with God. Yes, there are things you do not understand.

Yes, there are things you do not know what the future will be. Yes, there are things that right now, we do not even know how to answer, sit with them, and be silent with God. God is amid this, sitting with you. Accept mystery. Accept not knowing. Accept God's power into your life. Accept God's presence into your life." That means I do not have to understand everything.

Mary 'treasured all these words.' She thought about what all this meant. Then she 'pondered it in her heart.' She allowed it to sit within her.

If I was to go back over my faith journey through the years in the early days, I had no idea what life would become. I didn't realize the level of pain there would be in following God. Jesus said, "Pick up your cross and follow me."

There really is a cross to carry. I did not realize the miracles I would see with my own eyes. The things that I did not understand, how people have been healed of things, and circumstances changed. I could never have imagined the things God has done that I have seen with my own eyes.

I now look into the future, and I have confidence in God because I sat with God over a long period of time. But I have also learned to keep sitting because there is more and more.

It does not matter that you do not understand everything. It does not matter that everything does not make sense. Look for God in your life, train yourself to see and that it will influence us in this year.

It will help you start strong and to go deeper, not just into a new year or season, but for all future years. It will take you to a deeper place.

Mary is an example of someone who did not understand everything that was happening, but she treasured all the things of life that were happening, and God revealed himself.

If we look at Mary in the last stories of Mary in the Scriptures, and what has become known through the tradition about Mary in the church, it is amazing who she was, not just saying yes to Jesus, but the transformation in her life as she continued to sit with Jesus.

And it can be the same for you.

CHAPTER SEVENTEEN

FIFTEEN MINUTES A DAY

I f someone asked you what life is all about, you would have to say, life is all about 'becoming.' Becoming what? It's about becoming all that God planned for us to become.

The Bible puts this in religious language. It says that we are called to become like Christ because it says that we were made in the image and likeness of God. So, we are meant to become like Jesus himself in our life. We are meant to be in this relationship with God that is pure and loving. We are meant to live out the totality of who we are, constantly moving closer and closer to God and always becoming changed because of our encounter with God.

When I was younger, man, I had no idea what that meant. I thought that life was all about what I could do rather than realizing it was about what I could be. That God called me to become like Him.

Psalm 145 verse 18 says,

> The Lord is near to all who call on him, to all who
> call on him in truth.

In truth, the Lord is 'near.' Therefore, we are called to grow into this relationship with God.

God is close to whoever calls upon Him in honesty. The truth is the Lord is called to everybody, but not everybody acknowledges God.

Not everybody sees it. Not everybody understands it. So, if the Lord called all of us to be in this place where God has got space or room in our life, God has got to be able to come into our life.

The problem is that for so many of us, our life is so full of other things. God doesn't get a look in. God doesn't get space.

I remember when I was a younger man, someone who was teaching me to pray said to me, "What I want you to do is to pray for 15 minutes every day, not in the shower, not lying down, not in front of the television, 15 minutes a day, every day, don't miss." I remember saying, "That is ridiculous – 15 minutes of that. Where am I going to find 15 minutes a day?"

He used to say to me, "Whether you get up early, stay up late, study 15 minutes less or watch 15 minutes less of television. If you are meant to be becoming, if your relationship with God is meant to be the most important thing in your life, then make finding time to be with God a priority."

At the time, I used to think that was hard. It does not sound hard, but I remember he used to say, "15 minutes a day." The point is that over time, I learned that 15 minutes became a part of my life. The very reason I stand here today is that 15 minutes changed me, and I began to become more the person God called me to be.

Now, that is not my secret. But the truth is that within the teaching of the church, that within the Scriptures repeatedly, we 'become' by spending time with God.

We read in the Scriptures of Jesus so often going and spending time with the Father, being linked in and connected into God.

And so, I want to encourage you as we begin that you decide to spend time with God every day.

Now, if you do not know, I am a married guy. I have five children and I have ten grandchildren. I work in a ministry in a job that is tremendously busy. I cannot spend hours in prayer each day. I cannot spend hours reading my Bible or religious books every day.

It would be wrong if I did those things because God has asked something else of me. He has asked me and given me a vocation in terms of my life and what I am meant to be doing. So, I need to dedicate my life so that God could come into my life in those places and to be able to make space for God amid the things that He has asked me to do.

I want to encourage you to declutter your life sufficiently to make time for God, for you to have a personal heart-to-heart conversation with God every day. Pray on those days when you feel close to God and on those days when you do not feel close to God. The Scripture says the Lord is near to all who call on Him.

The Lord is with you, but you must call on Him and you call on Him in truth. "I am here. Speak to me, guide me, and lead me." I want to encourage you to find 15 minutes a day. It is not something you do with your wife or your husband. It is not something that you do with anyone else. It is a personal conversation between you and God every day. That is the way I was taught, and it has transformed my life and helped me to become more the person I am called to be.

Interestingly, the older I have become, the more I realize there is far more of me to become like God. When I was younger, I thought by the time I would get to be this age I would have it all together and would have a very deep relationship with God.

Indeed, while my relationship with God is far deeper than it was years ago, I have now realized there is more and more in this.

Declutter. Find time for God. Find space for God exactly where you are, and it will affect the totality of the rest of your life.

CHAPTER EIGHTEEN

FREEDOM THROUGH FORGIVENESS AND SORROW

Alll of us know that we are meant to be a certain kind of person and we are meant to do certain types of things based on our vocation, our stage in life, or where we are.

All of us know within us that there is a principle of right and wrong. All of us know in ourselves that to contravene certain rules and laws is what the Bible would call a sin, meaning we are turning away and turning our back on what God has called us to do.

Many of us want to 'become.' We have talked about 'becoming.' We have talked about seeing. We have talked about committing our plans to God. Many of us want to achieve and to 'become,' but there are things that happen in our life that diminish us that block the grace of God in our life. That is called sin. It is a rejection of God and we reject God by either what we call sins of commission, sins that we commit, or sins of omission, things that we should do, that we do not do. There are always consequences.

In James 4, verse 17, it says,

> *"Anyone who knows the right thing to do and fails to do it, commits sin."*

In other words, anyone who knows the right thing and fails to do it contravenes God's law, and to contravene that law separates us from God. Sin separates us from God.

Now, in Romans 6, verse 23, it says this,

> *For the wages of sin is death...*

What is a wage? A wage is something that you get for something that you have done.

> *For the wages of sin is death, but the free gift of God is eternal life in Christ Jesus, our Lord.*

In other words, it is saying that what you get for sin, what you get for rejecting God, is death. When we think of death, we think of dying. Dying in the Scriptures has an even more complex meaning.

It is not just the physical decay of our bodies, but death means to be separated from God, who is the source of all life. God, who is truth.

To be separated from that is to see us diminished within ourselves. The effect of sin is diminishing who we are, of who we are called to be.

Sin is the opposite of 'becoming.'

If we are to be the men and women that God called us to be, there are areas of our lives that we must stop and we have to say, 'I have got to address this. I have got to realize that I have got to stop doing some things. There are also things that I need to start doing because by not doing them, I am separating myself from God.'

It could be your language. It could be an attitude. It could be action.

It could be the way you love. It could be the things that you think about. It could be the way you care for things or respect things.

The way we do those things can diminish us and take us away from where God has called us to be.

When we come before God, it is an easy way to fix with two actions.

The first action is genuine forgiveness and sorrow. Forgiveness means saying, 'I have contravened your law, God.' Sorrow means saying, 'I have remorse within me; I'm going to change.' Forgiveness and sorrow go hand in hand so we can come before God and say, 'Lord, I have done these things. Forgive me. I feel genuine sorrow and I am going to change the way I do it.'

We have got to be careful. All of us are frail. All of us fall short. All of us need to be in the habit of coming before God and saying, 'Forgive me, I am sorry. I am going to do my best to change.'

The free gift of God is eternal life and so we can come back to God and ask over and over, 'Forgive me, forgive me, forgive me.' Then, when it is accompanied by this sorrow that says, 'I am going to do my best,' we can come into the presence of God and into the power of God in our life.

God is not looking for perfect people. God is looking for people who understand forgiveness and who have sorrow and decide they will try to not do it again in their life.

Where is it that you are being diminished? What are those areas?

What are you watching on television that takes away from being the man that God calls you to be? What is in your mind in terms of the things that you think about, your attitudes towards other people, the way you treat people, the way you treat the environment, the world around us, the way you are working, and the list goes on and on?

Where do you need to come before God and say, 'Forgive me, I am sorry to the point of I am going to change.' As we come before God and ask for forgiveness, I want to encourage you to say, 'God, forgive me. I want to change in the direction that you call me going right now.'

What you'll experience is freedom and the lifting of weight from you.

From a Catholic perspective, there is the sacrament of reconciliation or confession. For many people, it is out of fashion to the degree that people do not really understand what it really is. I appreciate that.

For many of you who are not Catholic, it may be something you don't recognize.

Repentance is a gift where we receive grace to be changed and to be transformed and reconnected into a community.

It is God who forgives sin and God who restores us to new life.

CHAPTER NINETEEN

GOD'S BLESSING IS COMING

How we set up our relationship with God and press into God will affect every aspect of our lives. The Scriptures tell us that we should have plans for our life and the direction we want to go.

Something very important to do is bringing your needs before God and asking for God's help.

When I was an immature Christian person, whenever I started to pray, it did not take me very long and it almost immediately went to asking God, 'Can I have this girl? Can I have that? Can you do this? Can you do that? Can you bless them? Can you fix that? And my whole prayer life with God, if I was honest, was all about asking God for things.

If your relationship with anybody is all about just asking, it is not a terribly healthy relationship. So, one of the things I say to my staff when we pray together is 'praise before please.' It is acknowledging God for who God is, the attributes of God, the character of God, the gifts of God and the blessings that God gives us. It is acknowledging all of that before we come and put our needs before God. So, 'praise before please' is basically saying to God, 'I acknowledge who you are.' Once we have done that, you can come before God and bring your needs before God because one of the things that is very clear – God wants to give us things. In the beginning, God made us that we would share in His very life.

In the Sermon on the Mount in Matthew 7, verse 7, Jesus is speaking to the people on the mountain, and He says this to them,

> *"Ask, and it will be given to you, search and you will find, knock and the door will be opened to you for everyone who asks, receives, and everyone who searches finds. And for everyone who knocks the door will be opened. Is there any among you who, if your child asks for bread will give a stone, or if the child asks for a fish will give a snake? If you then who are evil, know how to give good gifts to your children? How much more will your Father in heaven give good things to those who ask him?"*

Jesus is saying, 'Ask.' The act of asking is an act of praise when done in the right relationship to acknowledging God with praise before, please. It is an act of worship and it is an act of honor.

When we bring our needs before God, we are effectively saying, 'God, there are all these things that I can't do. There are these things that I believe that you've called me or want me to do or how to live. These urges and desires within me are not necessarily bad things but things I would like to achieve. So, I am asking for your blessing to come into my life and for your work to come into my life.'

When we do that, we effectively acknowledge God. We are saying,' God, you are greater than me.'

In the Personal Prayer book that I wrote on how to pray, the very first action of prayer is what I call Perspective. Perspective means to understand something in light of something else. When I know God and His greatness and His majesty, who He is and that He made us and holds us in the Palm of His hand and then I come before God with my needs, I'm saying to God, I acknowledge who you are and so Perspective is critical.

I want to encourage you right now. What are the things that you believe God is putting on your heart?

Why don't you bring your needs before God, whether it be for relationships, whether it be for health, whether it be in your work career, your family, for your children, for the world?

Why don't you bring those before God and ask God for His blessing upon them? I really want to encourage you to do something if you're going to build your faith. No matter how outrageous or outlandish they are, write down those prayer requests and pray for them regularly.

The benefit of writing them down is that you will remember and, in the future, when you see how God has worked in those situations. You will be able to look back and it will build your faith.

God does not give us everything we want because sometimes we do not understand the whole picture. There are many things I have prayed for, and God did not give me and thank the Lord that He did not.

I want to encourage you to offer your requests in prayer to God. I will join you in prayer if you email your prayer requests to me at this email address: prayer@BruceDownes.org. I would love to pray for you.

As Christians, our goal is to grow closer to God in our everyday lives. As you get closer to God, you begin to resemble God more in how you live, think and love. With God, you can start strong and thrive in any season in life.